Little People, **BIG DREAMS**™
MARY EARPS

Written by
Maria Isabel Sánchez Vegara

Illustrated by
Ana Gomez

Frances Lincoln
Children's Books

In a town near Nottingham, there lived a lively girl
named Mary. She loved dancing, swimming, running . . .
But her favorite pastime was joining her dad
and brother, Joel, to kick a ball around.

Mary was ten when she joined her first real team.
She started as a midfielder but also tried other positions.
One Saturday, while defending the goal, she saved a penalty.
That's when she realized she had a talent for goalkeeping!

Soccer really changed things for Mary! It made her feel more confident and helped her make friends. At school, she found talking with others easier and was no longer shy about speaking up in class debates.

When Mary was fourteen, Leicester City offered her a place at their training center for promising players. As she defended her new team's goal, she dreamed of turning pro and playing in the Women's Super League.

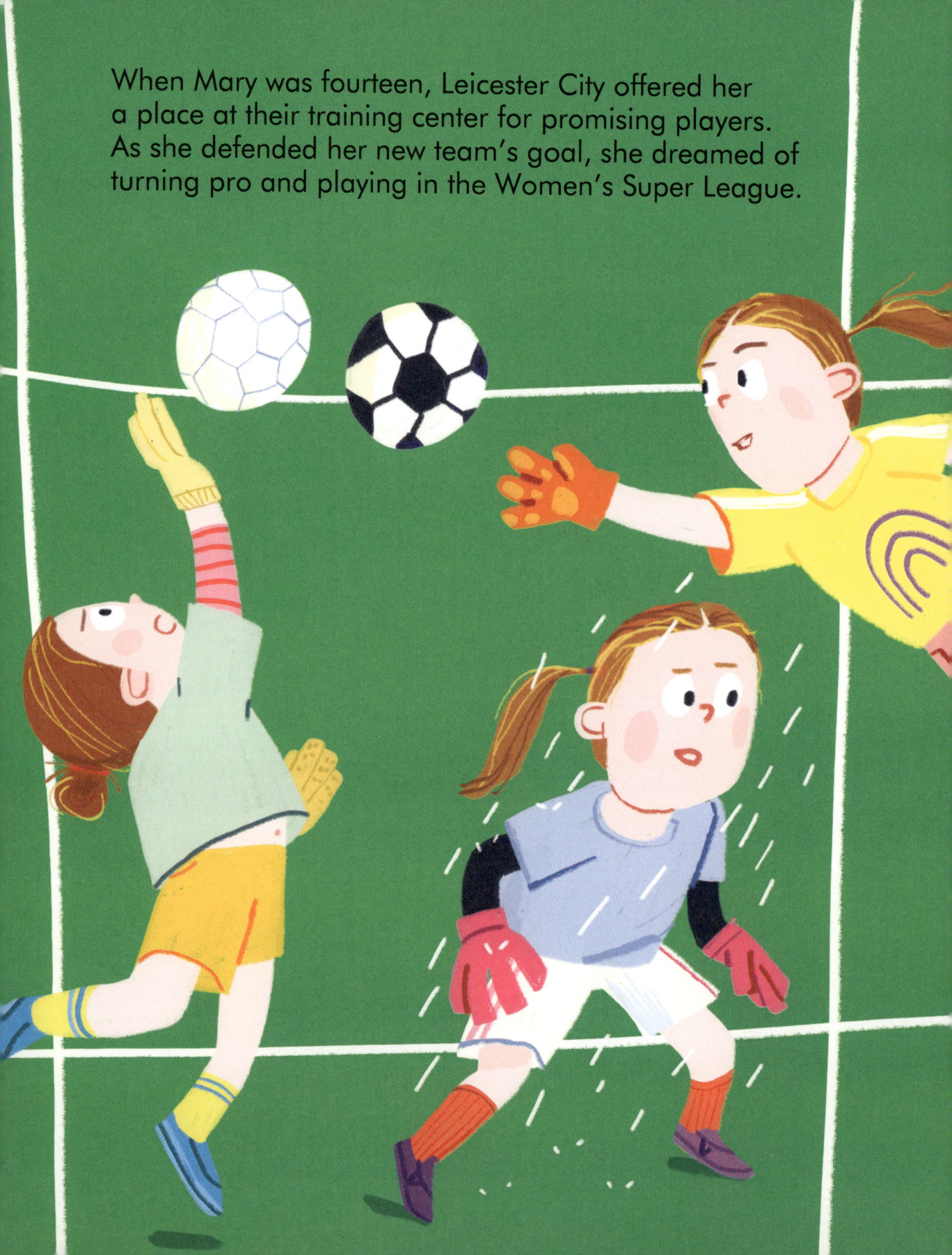

But in England's top women's league, it could take a player a year to earn what a male soccer player earned in a week! So, Mary decided it would be safer to go to university in case she had to get a second job to pay the bills.

Upon graduating, Mary made it into England's senior squad, The Lionesses. She was her country's fourth-string goalkeeper, but that didn't make her family any less proud.

She also proved herself playing for a German team. After Mary helped her club win Germany's top league, Manchester United asked her to be their goalie. Life felt good!

But everything changed when she was suddenly dropped from the England team. To make matters worse, her new contract from Manchester United wouldn't pay enough. Mary thought her soccer days were over. She had never felt so low!

Luckily, her family and friends were there to cheer her up, and her club agreed to raise her pay a little. Then came Sarina Wiegman, the new national coach, who believed in Mary and offered her a chance to play for England again.

A year later, the Lionesses became European Champions! Soon after, Mary and her teammates wrote a letter to the government. They wanted every school in the UK to give girls the same opportunities as boys to play soccer.

The following summer, thirteen million England fans tuned in to watch Mary save a penalty in the Women's World Cup final in Australia. Although the Lionesses ended up losing, back home they were welcomed as champions.

Mary was voted the world's best goalkeeper, won the BBC Sports Personality award, and received a special honor from William, Prince of Wales. Everyone wanted to thank her for helping put women's soccer in the spotlight.

Having become the first goalkeeper to achieve 50 clean sheets in the Women's Super League, Mary decided to leave Manchester United and join Paris Saint-Germain. But she remained a Lioness, always ready to defend the England goal.

And the "Queen of Stops" has a message for all those who face challenges on the path to their dream:

Sometimes success is not about collecting trophies. It's about waking up and putting one foot in front of the other.

MARY EARPS

(Born 1993)

2011

2017

Born in Nottinghamshire, Mary Earps was eight when she began joining her dad and brother in the backyard to play soccer. Two years later, she joined a local team and quickly realized that she belonged in the goal. By 2019, Mary was living her dream, playing for Manchester United and the senior England squad. But her hopes were dashed when she was later dropped from the national team. She became so disheartened that she almost quit the sport altogether, but her family and friends encouraged her to keep trying. To Mary's delight, a new England coach, Sarina Wiegman, saw her talent and asked her to come back. With Mary defending the goal, the Lionesses won the 2022 European Championship, gaining fans and inspiring many girls to start playing. The public fell in love with Mary's

2022   2024

energy and confidence, giving her the nickname "Queen of Stops."
Soon after, she was awarded BBC Sports Personality of the Year, FIFA
Women's Goalkeeper of the Year, an honorary doctorate, and an MBE—
and even has a tram named after her in Nottingham! Off the field, Mary
feels strongly about giving girls and women equal opportunities in sports.
She urged the UK government to add girls' soccer to the school curriculum
and called out a major sponsor for not printing the women's goalkeeper
shirt ahead of the 2023 World Cup. When the sponsor finally offered the
shirt, it sold out in five minutes! Mary's story reminds us that through the
ups and downs we should never stop believing in ourselves. As Mary says:
"There's only one of you in the world, and that's more than good enough."

Want to find out more?

Have a read of these great books:

Earps (Ultimate Football Heroes) by Emily Stead

The Rise of the Lionesses: Incredible Moments from Women's Football
by Flo Lloyd-Hughes

To my friend Chelsea, let your light shine bright!

First published in the U.S. in 2025 by Frances Lincoln Children's Books, an imprint of The Quarto Group.
100 Cummings Center, Suite 265D, Beverly, MA 01915, USA.
T +1 978-282-9590 F +1 078-283-2742 www.Quarto.com

ISBN 978-1-83600-658-9
Set in Futura BT.

Published by Peter Marley · Edited by Molly Mead
Designed by Sasha Moxon and Izzy Bowman
Production by Robin Boothroyd
Manufactured in Guangdong, China CC012025
1 3 5 7 9 8 6 4 2

Photographic acknowledgments (pages 28-29, from left to right): 1. Mary Earps of Doncaster Rovers Belles FC looks on during
the FA Women's Super League match between Chelsea Ladies FC and Doncaster Rovers Belles FC at Tooting & Mitcham United on
July 31, 2011 in London, England © Tom Dulat – The FA/The FA Collection via Getty Images. 2. Goalkeeper Mary Earps during an
England Women's senior team training session on July 31, 2017 in Utrecht, Netherlands © Catherine Ivill – AMA/Getty Images Sport/
Getty Images Europe via Getty Images. 3. England's goalkeeper Mary Earps celebrates on the final whistle in the UEFA Women's
Euro 2022 Group A football match between England and Austria at Old Trafford in Manchester, north-west England on July 6, 2022,
England won the game 1–0 © Daniel MIHAILESCU/AFP via Getty Images. 4. Mary Earps of Paris Saint-Germain takes a selfie for
spectators following the Perth International Football Cup match between West Ham United and Paris Saint-Germain at HBF Park
on August 29, 2024 in Perth, Australia © Paul Kane/Stringer/Getty Images AsiaPac via Getty Images.

Collect the Little People, BIG DREAMS™ series:

FRIDA KAHLO 	COCO CHANEL	MAYA ANGELOU 	AMELIA EARHART	AGATHA CHRISTIE 	MARIE CURIE 	ROSA PARKS 	AUDREY HEPBURN 	EMMELINE PANKHURST 
ELLA FITZGERALD	ADA LOVELACE 	JANE AUSTEN 	GEORGIA O'KEEFFE 	HARRIET TUBMAN 	ANNE FRANK 	MOTHER TERESA 	JOSEPHINE BAKER 	L. M. MONTGOMERY 
JANE GOODALL 	SIMONE DE BEAUVOIR 	MUHAMMAD ALI 	STEPHEN HAWKING 	MARIA MONTESSORI 	VIVIENNE WESTWOOD 	MAHATMA GANDHI 	DAVID BOWIE 	WILMA RUDOLPH 
DOLLY PARTON 	BRUCE LEE 	RUDOLF NUREYEV 	ZAHA HADID 	MARY SHELLEY 	MARTIN LUTHER KING JR. 	DAVID ATTENBOROUGH 	ASTRID LINDGREN 	EVONNE GOOLAGONG 
BOB DYLAN 	ALAN TURING 	BILLIE JEAN KING 	GRETA THUNBERG	JESSE OWENS	JEAN-MICHEL BASQUIAT	ARETHA FRANKLIN	CORAZON AQUINO	PELÉ
ERNEST SHACKLETON	STEVE JOBS	AYRTON SENNA	LOUISE BOURGEOIS	ELTON JOHN	JOHN LENNON	PRINCE	CHARLES DARWIN	CAPTAIN TOM MOORE
HANS CHRISTIAN ANDERSEN 	STEVIE WONDER	MEGAN RAPINOE 	MARY ANNING	MALALA YOUSAFZAI 	ANDY WARHOL 	RUPAUL	MICHELLE OBAMA	MINDY KALING
IRIS APFEL	ROSALIND FRANKLIN	RUTH BADER GINSBURG 	MARILYN MONROE 	KAMALA HARRIS 	ALBERT EINSTEIN	CHARLES DICKENS 	YOKO ONO 	MICHAEL JORDAN

NELSON MANDELA PABLO PICASSO AMANDA GORMAN GLORIA STEINEM FLORENCE NIGHTINGALE HARRY HOUDINI J.R.R. TOLKIEN ELVIS PRESLEY NEIL ARMSTRONG

ALEXANDER VON HUMBOLDT NIKOLA TESLA WILMA MANKILLER MARCUS RASHFORD LAVERNE COX MAE JEMISON DWAYNE JOHNSON HELEN KELLER ANNA PAVLOVA

QUEEN ELIZABETH TERRY FOX HEDY LAMARR SHAKIRA FREDDIE MERCURY LEWIS HAMILTON LOUIS PASTEUR PRINCESS DIANA DAVID HOCKNEY

VANESSA NAKATE OLIVE MORRIS KING CHARLES MOZART STEVE IRWIN JÜRGEN KLOPP LEO MESSI SALLY RIDE TENZING NORGAY

KYLIE MINOGUE BEYONCÉ TAYLOR SWIFT RAFA NADAL USAIN BOLT SIMONE BILES STAN LEE LEONARD COHEN VINCENT VAN GOGH

MARY KOM SALVADOR DALÍ ANTOINE DE SAINT-EXUPÉRY DAVID BECKHAM KATHERINE JOHNSON PATRICK MAHOMES

YAYOI KUSAMA ROALD DAHL HARRY STYLES WILLIAM KAMKWAMBA MARY EARPS

Scan the QR code for free activity sheets, teachers' notes and more information about the series at www.littlepeoplebigdreams.com